FOR SiNGING OUT LOUD!

SpongeBob's
Book of
Showstopping
Jokes

Stephen Hillenburg

Based on the TV series *SpongeBob SquarePants*® created by Stephen Hillenburg as seen on Nickelodeon®

ISBN-13: 978-0-545-04146-1
ISBN-10: 0-545-04146-5

12 11 10 9 8 7 6 5 4 3 2 1   8 9 10 11 12 13/0

Printed in the U.S.A.

First Scholastic printing, January 2008

FOR SINGING OUT LOUD!

SpongeBob's Book of Showstopping Jokes

by David Lewman

SCHOLASTIC INC.

New York Toronto London Auckland Sydney
Mexico City New Delhi Hong Kong Buenos Aires

ROCK ON, SPONGEBOB!

- ★ **FAVORITE SONG:** "THE GARY IN THE SHELL"
- ★ **BEST MOVE:** TEARING MYSELF IN HALF
- ★ **WHAT I SHOUT AT THE END OF MY SONG:** "THANK YOU, BIKINI BOTTOM!"
- ★ **MOST EMBARRASSING TALENT SHOW MOMENT:** GOT THE MICROPHONE STUCK IN ONE OF MY HEAD HOLES

HOT TIPS

1. DO absorb a lot of water before you sing.

2. DON'T sing before you're READY!

3. DO make sure your shoes are shined and your tie is tied just right.

4. DON'T let Plankton trick you into singing the Krabby Patty recipe.

5. DO finish by floating away in a giant bubble.

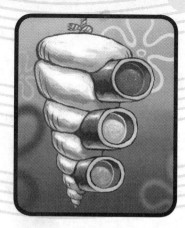

Patrick: How did the traffic light do in the talent contest?

SpongeBob: He stopped the show!

Why did Mrs. Puff bake bread for the talent show?

Because there's no business like dough business.

Why did Plankton enter the talent contest?

He wanted to steal the show.

What do you call a singing contest for ghosts?

Scary-oke.

Patrick: Why did the jellyfish enter the talent show?

SpongeBob: He thought it was a stinging contest.

What's it called when SpongeBob sings at boating school?

A class act.

Patrick: What kind of furniture is best at talent shows?

SpongeBob: Musical chairs.

Does SpongeBob like dancing?

Yes, he gets a real kick out of it.

Sandy: Which tune is the sweetest?

Pearl: The caramel-ody.

What key is it best to sing in at the zoo?

Mon-key.

SpongeBob: What do you call a dancing rock?

Patrick: A stepping stone.

9

YOU'RE A STAR, PATRICK!

★ **FAVORITE SONG:** "ROCK-A-BYE, PATRICK"

★ **BEST MOVE:** THE BLANK STARE

★ **WHAT I SHOUT AT THE END OF MY SONG:**

"UH . . . I THINK I'M DONE."

★ **MOST EMBARRASSING TALENT SHOW MOMENT:**

REALIZED I WAS ONSTAGE

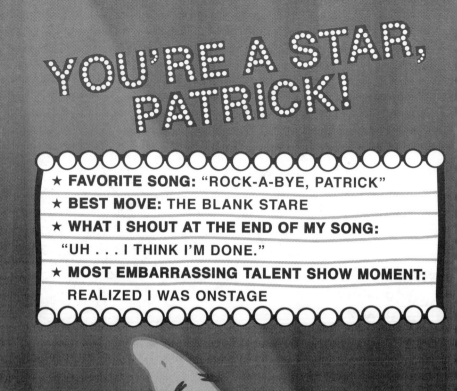

HOT TIPS

1. DO bring something to eat during your song.

2. DON'T mistake the microphone for a hot dog.

3. DON'T sing with your mouth full.

4. DO wear something over your underwear.

5. DO make sure your underwear is clean.

SpongeBob: Which singers are the cleanest?

Squidward: The soap-ranos.

Patrick: Who sings even higher than a tenor?

Plankton: An eleven-or.

SpongeBob: How do you make sure the audience can hear you?

Patrick: Wear a really loud outfit.

Mrs. Puff: What kind of song do electric eels sing?

Mr. Krabs: Shock 'n' roll.

SpongeBob: What kind of song do parrots sing?

Painty the Pirate: Squawk 'n' roll.

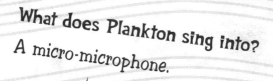

What does Plankton sing into?
A micro-microphone.

Why isn't Squidward friendly with his dance coach?

They started off on the wrong foot.

SpongeBob: Is it true that the dancers gave up?

Sandy: Yes, they threw in the twirl!

Sandy: What's the difference between a statue and an unsure singer?

SpongeBob: One's white marble and the other might warble.

Why did Plankton sweep up his footprints on the way to the talent show?

So he'd be a hard act to follow!

Why did Patrick bring a vegetable to the talent show?

He wanted to feel the beet.

Why did Patrick bring a baseball to the singing contest?

He'd heard it was important to stay on pitch.

TAKE IT AWAY, SQUIDWARD!

★ **FAVORITE SONG:** "I WANT TO HOLD YOUR HAND, HAND, HAND, HAND, HAND, HAND"

★ **BEST MOVE:** AWAY FROM SPONGEBOB

★ **WHAT I SHOUT AT THE END OF MY SONG:** "YOU PEOPLE WOULDN'T KNOW GOOD MUSIC IF IT STARED YOU IN THE FACE!"

★ **MOST EMBARRASSING TALENT SHOW MOMENT:** FOUND OUT THAT PEOPLE WOULD RATHER WATCH SPONGEBOB SWEEP THE STAGE

HOT TIPS

1. DO study classical music for years and years and years.

2. DON'T expect Bikini Bottom dwellers to appreciate it.

3. DO exactly as I do.

4. DON'T let SpongeBob talk you into practicing with him.

5. DO applaud loudly for me when I win.

Why did SpongeBob practice his arithmetic before the singing contest?

He'd heard you have to be really good at your addition.

Why did Sandy visit the Texas desert before the singing contest?

She'd heard that cactus makes perfect.

Why was SpongeBob scared to enter the singing contest?

He'd heard that first you have to make it through the dry-outs.

Why did Patrick sleep under his songs?

He'd heard they were sheet music.

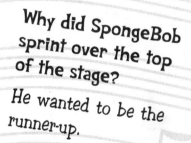

Why did SpongeBob sprint over the top of the stage?

He wanted to be the runner-up.

SpongeBob: Who's second-in-command at singing contests?

Sandy: The voice president.

What kind of tuba does Patrick practice on every night?

A tuba toothpaste.

Squidward: Why do cymbals make bad drivers?

Mrs. Puff: They're always crashing!

Barnacleboy: Why was the reporter arrested at the music contest?

Mermaidman: He kept taking notes.

SpongeBob: Why aren't stingrays good singers?

Squidward: They're always flat.

Patrick: Why aren't swordfish good singers?

Sandy: They're always sharp.

Why did Patrick bring birthday paper to the singing contest?

He wanted to be a wrapper.

HOWDY, SANDY!

- ★ **FAVORITE SONG:** "GIT ALONG, LITTLE DOGFISH"
- ★ **BEST MOVE:** EXTREME MICROPHONE-STAND TWIRLING
- ★ **WHAT I SHOUT AT THE END OF MY SONG:** "THAT ONE'S FOR TEXAS!"
- ★ **MOST EMBARRASSING TALENT SHOW MOMENT:** ACCIDENTALLY LASSOED ONE OF THE JUDGES

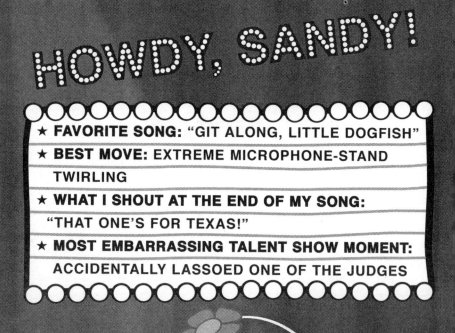

HOT TIPS

1. DO warm up with a cowgirl yell: "YEE-HAH!"

2. DON'T forget to wear your air helmet if you're singing underwater (and you're a land critter).

3. DO remember to smile and show your big front teeth.

4. DON'T dare to sing a song about Texas unless you're FROM the great state of Texas.

5. DO work out before, after, and during your song.

What does SpongeBob sing to his Krabby Patties at bedtime?

A lullafry.

What's the name of SpongeBob's choir?

The Porous Chorus.

SpongeBob: What's huge, stomps around, and sings beautifully?

Sandy: Tyrannochorus rex.

Patrick: The judge said I sing like a baritone!

Squidward: No, he said he can't bear your tone.

Sandy: The judge said my voice was great!

Squidward: No, he said your voice was grating.

Chum Bucket

What is Plankton calling his new store for percussion instruments?

The Drum Bucket.

Patrick: Who brings you money when you lose your horn?

SpongeBob: The toot fairy.

Did Plankton meet the dance judge's standards?

No, he fell short.

Did SpongeBob enjoy playing the trumpet?

Yes, he had a blast.

How did Patrick get caught in a drum?

It was a snare drum.

Why did Patrick build a bonfire before the singing contest?

He'd heard it was important to warm up.

Patrick: How'd the firecracker do at the singing contest?

SpongeBob: Great—he burst into a pop song.

SING IT, EUGENE!

- ★ **FAVORITE SONG:** "I'VE GOT YOUR MONEY IN MY HANDS"
- ★ **BEST MOVE:** SPOTTING STRAY COINS ON THE STAGE
- ★ **WHAT I SHOUT AT THE END OF MY SONG:** "EAT AT THE KRUSTY KRAB!"
- ★ **MOST EMBARRASSING TALENT SHOW MOMENT:** MISTOOK JUDGE'S SHINY BUTTON FOR A QUARTER AND DOVE FOR IT

HOT TIPS

1. DO eat plenty of Krabby Patties before the contest.

2. DON'T expect to get free napkins.

3. DO tell all your friends to eat at the Krusty Krab.

4. DON'T ever eat at the Chum Bucket.

5. DO celebrate winning (or losing) with a big platter of delicious Krabby Patties.

How did SpongeBob's song go over at Mussel Beach?

He got a sandy ovation.

Pearl: Why was the student disappointed with the key the judge picked for him?

Mrs. Puff: He got an F.

Squidward: What do you call a group of nervous musicians?

Mr. Krabs: A sweatband.

Why did SpongeBob's boss take up the violin?

He wanted to be a fiddler crab.

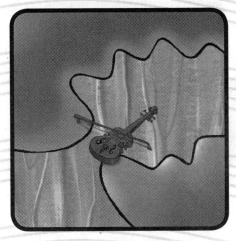

Sandy: What did the big wind tell the little wind before she sang?

SpongeBob: "Just remember to breeze."

Patrick: What kind of singing voice does corn have?

Plankton: Husky.

Why did Patrick climb up on the roof before he sang?

The judge told him to take it from the top.

Squidward: How did the mouse do in the singing contest?

Sandy: He squeaked through it.

SpongeBob: Why don't eggs sing high notes?

Mr. Krabs: They always crack.

Patrick: How did the pony do in the singing contest?

SpongeBob: He was a little hoarse.

Pearl: What musical instrument do geometry teachers like best?

Mrs. Puff: Triangles.

TELL IT LIKE IT IS, SHELDON!

★ **FAVORITE SONG:** "IF YOU'RE EVIL AND YOU KNOW IT, RAISE YOUR HAND"

★ **BEST MOVE:** RAISING BOTH ARMS AND LAUGHING MANIACALLY

★ **WHAT I SHOUT AT THE END OF MY SONG:** "BOW DOWN AND DO MY BIDDING!"

★ **MOST EMBARRASSING TALENT SHOW MOMENT:** COULDN'T REACH THE MICROPHONE

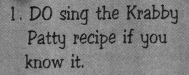

HOT TIPS

1. DO sing the Krabby Patty recipe if you know it.

2. DON'T expect to win if I'm competing.

3. DO build a remote-controlled robot to sing your song for you.

4. DON'T get in my way.

5. DO bribe the judges—but not with food from the Chum Bucket. (It doesn't work, believe me).

SpongeBob: How did the sledgehammer do in the contest?

Patrick: He was a smashing success.

Why did Patrick click his fingers through his whole song?

The judge told him to make it snappy.

Plankton: Why did the professional chef win the singing contest?

SpongeBob: He had a big range.

36

Pearl: Knock, knock.
Mrs. Puff: Who's there?
Pearl: Al.
Mrs. Puff: Al who?
Pearl: Altos over here, sopranos over there.

Why do chickens make good percussionists?

They're born with two drumsticks.

Patrick: Are high notes good?

Squidward: No, they're nothing but treble.

What's SpongeBob's favorite musical instrument?

The fry-olin.

Plankton: What kind of music always stinks?

SpongeBob: Reek 'n' roll.

Sandy: What kind of music is best for a ship at the bottom of the ocean?

Squidward: Wreck 'n' roll.

Mrs. Puff: What kind of music do rabbits like best?
Sandy: Hip-hop.

Squidward: What do you call a very short song sung by a cat?
Sandy: An itty-bitty kitty ditty

39

HELLOOOO, MRS. PUFF!

★ **FAVORITE SONG:** "MY STUDENTS DRIVE UNDER THE OCEAN"

★ **BEST MOVE:** KEEPING TIME WITH A POINTER

★ **WHAT I SHOUT AT THE END OF MY SONG:** "NOW BACK TO CLASS!"

★ **MOST EMBARRASSING TALENT SHOW MOMENT:** I WAS SO NERVOUS I INFLATED IN THE MIDDLE OF MY SONG

HOT TIPS

1. DO study your lyrics carefully.

2. DON'T let SpongeBob drive you to the show.

3. DO wear a new hat.

4. DON'T ask Patrick to accompany you.

5. DO give your music teacher lots of presents.

SpongeBob: Why are fish such good musicians?

Mrs. Puff: They're always polishing their scales.

Sandy: How did the wrecking ball do in the singing contest?

Squidward: He brought the house down.

What happened to SpongeBob and Patrick's plans for dancing on a paper stage?

They fell through.

Squidward: How is a good dancer like a stairway?

Sandy: They're both full of steps.

Mr. Krabs: Why do math teachers always enter singing contests?

Mrs. Puff: They love to do their numbers.

Why didn't Patrick take the free guitar?

He heard there were strings attached.

SpongeBob: Do guitars get teased a lot?

Sandy: Yes, they're always getting picked on.

Patrick: What has wings and plays the guitar?

Mr. Krabs: The strummingbird.

Why did Squidward play a drum for the talent show judges?

They told him to beat it.

SpongeBob: Which musical instrument is the hardest to see?

Mr. Krabs: The foghorn.

SpongeBob: Which pet is the most musical?

Sandy: The trumpet.

Mermaidman: Why do violins make good presents?

Barnacleboy: They always come with a bow.

IT'S ALL ABOUT YOU, PEARL!

★ **FAVORITE SONG:** "HOW MUCH IS THAT OUTFIT IN THE WINDOW?"

★ **BEST MOVE:** THE POUT

★ **WHAT I SHOUT AT THE END OF MY SONG:** "SIT DOWN, DADDY!"

★ **MOST EMBARRASSING TALENT SHOW MOMENT:** DADDY JUMPED ONSTAGE AND SHOUTED, "THAT'S MY BABY!"

HOT TIPS

1. DO get all your friends to cheer for you.

2. DON'T let SpongeBob come up with your dance moves.

3. DO wear your hair in a ponytail.

4. DO throw an after-party.

5. DON'T throw it at the Krusty Krab.

Why did Patrick finish his song by whacking a drum?

He wanted to go out with a bang!